Oracle Bones

Oracle Bones

poems by
C. Mikal Oness

LEWIS-CLARK PRESS

LEWIS-CLARK BOOKS
EXPEDITION AWARD WINNER FOR 2006

Published by Lewis-Clark Press
Lewiston, ID 83501, U.S.A.

Copyright © 2007 by C. Mikal Oness
All rights reserved

p. cm.

ISBN 0-911015-63-9
ISBN 978-0-911015-63-8

Library of Congress Cataloging-in-Publication Data
Oness, C. Mikal.--
Oracle bones / C. Mikal Oness

Printed in the United States of America
Set in Bembo
Designed by Kimberly Verhines and Mark Sanders
Cover design by Emily Perkins, Sean Watkins, and Mark Sanders

Except in the United States of America, this book is sold subject to the condition that it shall not, by way of trade or otherwise, be lent, re-sold, hired out, or otherwise circulated without the publisher's prior consent in any form of binding or cover other than that in which it is published.

ACKNOWLEDGMENTS:

Special thanks to the editors of the following magazines in which many of these poems first appeared, sometimes in earlier versions or under different titles:

American Literary Review: "Aubade for Brenda"
Black Warrior Review: "August 1990"
The Colorado Review: "Swallows" and "No Name"
The Connecticut Review: "Enskyment" and "The Tongues of Water"
Fence: "Birth of the Father" and "Posse" ("Ye Rosebuds for an old nickel")
Great River Review: "Poem for the Holidays" and "Poetry of Witness"
The Iowa Review: "Return," "A Sort of Hunger," and "Eulogia"
The Journal: "Next Dream"
The Marlboro Review: "Charm"
Meridian: "Runian I-V," "Sorbies," and "Chisel"
The Montserrat Review: "In Memoriam"
Poet Lore: "Poetry as a Way of Talking to the Self" and "Poetry as a Way of Talking to Others"
Puerto del Sol: "Were I This Forest Pool"
Rattle: "Apologia" and "How to Deserve"
Rivendell: "Sea Voyage"
Shenandoah: "Ready," "Struck," "Moon and Sun," "Stealth" ("Down in the reeds"), "Stealth" ("We're told that rain brings them up"), "Reverdie," and "The Handworm's Hipbone"
Solo: A Journal of Poetry: "Garden Elegy"
South Coast Poetry Review: "Not Grace Exactly"
Third Coast: "Circe's This Craft"
Two Rivers Review: "Forever"
What Light: "Elegy" and "Scapulimancy"
Whirligig: A Journal of Language Arts: "Wild Elegy"
WV: "Divide, Divide"

"Eulogia" also appears in *Husks* from Brandenburg Press, 1998.

"Moon and Sun," "Runian I-V," and "Posse" ("Can you finish can you be burned together can you wake") appear in a limited edition artist book, *Runian*, and as a suite of broadsides from Bergamot Press.

"August 1990" appears in *The Geography of Home: California and the Poetry of Place* (Hey Day Books).

Special thanks to George Mason University for the Mary Roberts Rinehart Award in Poetry given to some of these poems and for the support it therefore gave to write more of them. Thanks are also due to the Wisconsin Arts Board who awarded a grant for many of these poems.

The "Runian" sequence is for Terrell Beck; 'Verse' is for Pamela McClure; Sonja, in "Begin with a Machine" is Sonja Simonson Schrag; "Swallows" is for Tom Stroik; "Old English Poem" is for John Miles Foley; "Soul Travel" is for Ernie Merritt; "Mother's Day" is for Elizabeth Oness; "No Name" is for Boyd White who has come greatly to my aid. Thanks to Gary Young, Boyd White and Pamela McClure for their editorial guidance and great friendship.

From *Beowulf*, translated by Burton Raffel, copyright © 1963 renewed © 1991 by Burton Raffel. Used by permission of Dutton Signet, a division of Penguin Group (USA) Inc.

"I Want to Sleep" by Jorge Guillen, trans. James Wright, *Collected Poems* (Wesleyan University Press, 1971). © 1971 by James Wright and reprinted by permission of Wesleyan University Press.

CONTENTS

The Handworm's Hipbone / 13

I *Divinations*
August 1990 / 17
Return / 18
Ready / 18
The Sorbies / 19
Make an Offer / 20
On Wood or Bone / 20
Chisel / 21
Apologia / 23
Forever / 23
Elegy / 24
Devotion / 25
Birth of the Father / 25
Sea Voyage / 26
Ever Ending / 28
Eulogia / 28
Aubade for Brenda / 29
Never Experience / 30
In Memoriam / 31
Circe's This Craft / 32
Poetry as a Way of Talking to Others / 34
Stealth / 34
Posse / 35

II *Scapulimancy*
Divide, Divide / 39
Privilege / 40
Old English Poem / 41
Another Old English Poem / 41
Reverdie / 42
Mother's Day / 42
Struck / 43
Ever Ending / 43
Runian / 44

Scapulimancy / 45
Mantra / 45
How to Deserve / 46
Poetry as a Way of Talking to the Self / 46
Ever Ending / 47
You, Your Mother, and I / 47
Begin with a Machine / 48
To Step Out of My Heart / 48
Posse / 49

    I I I *Charms*
Trisomy 18 / 53
Missouri Summer / 54
What Is Rare / 55
Reincarnation / 56
Poetry as a Way of Talking to Spirit / 57
A Sort of Hunger / 57
Were I this Forest Pool / 58
Blood Trout / 58
Com on Wanre Niht / 59
Moon and Sun / 59
In Swaying Copse the Willows / 60
Stealth / 60
Mentor / 61
Poem for the Holidays / 62
The Tongues of Water / 63
Verse / 63
Next Dream / 64
Enskyment / 65
No Name / 65
Oracle Bones / 66
Posse / 67
Charm / 68

For Beth

ORACLE BONES

The Handworm's Hipbone

He þe sceal legge   leaf et heafde.

Under the overturned wheelbarrow,
   in the dark of that insulated space
warmed by the decay of last year's leaves,
   is the dark of the dark and building soil,
is the dark of the ever-dampening.

And when I overturned the overturned
   wheelbarrow, the dark flew out like a covey,
like sparrows, and having been for so long
   so used to all of its damp and warm
containment, and having fled so quickly,

it left behind the decayed, or half-decayed
   body of an ordinary bird, a black bird,
the remnants of its red brassards browning
   beside it. The remnants of last year's leaves
also lain by its head for so long as to be

blackening beside it, silent and benign,
   as if sent there by charm to diminish
some inconsequential thing shamefully
   placed in a dark space in a dark time
to become naught in the heart of the harrower.

I

Divinations

> *High up over his head they flew*
> *His shining banner, then sadly let*
> *The water pull at the ship, watched it*
> *Slowly sliding to where neither rulers*
> *Nor heroes nor anyone can say whose hands*
> *Opened to take that motionless cargo.*
>
> *Beowulf* (ll. 47-52), Burton Raffel, trans.

August 1990

I sit too still and think about five years
ago in Santa Barbara. My niece
to do her first ballet, and that day Don
and I arrange for brunch at the Upham Inn
before I go to see Kell dance; I dream
the night before of bringing her a rose.
And it seems now as if brunch were a dream—
a fourteen dollar plate of shrimp and ham,
champagne from ten to twelve, and staggering
to my car. What did we talk about? Our jobs?
I loved Don's Nietschzean plume of a moustache,
his balding head, his years above my own.
I loved his craft—rail caps he made on the boat
gleamed with my varnishings each day; they were
his lips glinting with scotch; they were my lips.
I only remember this: a sharp right turn;
in retrospect, a dreadful look of horror
on a woman's face; then time goes past; I wake
to a loud slide, a crash of glass; my dash
board spins; I fall against the roof, the road
through the open window; I pull myself
out of my car, I think; I walk myself
past Donny, past a full crowd looking on.
I was, I say. I drove. It was me driving.
Yes, yes, yes, yes. I understand. I'm fine.
And powerless—that's what it is you know—
on the curb pulling my ripped shirt over
my head, refusing help from the paramedics—
I am refusing help for the last time.
Because years later walking down the street,
or sitting on my bed at night, it comes
to me that I have done this, and someone
is dead, and that a mother must still weep
just north of here; I can begin to hear
her now. I can begin just now.

Return

The door I tape up in fall
   I untape now and open
and sift dust across the sill,
     bare-grey, burnished, ashen.

Ready

Ready the wings; ready the dew beads;
   ready the iron pincers; ready the fire;
ready the mist; ready the pinched heads
   of rosemary, the mead, the banjo, the lyre.
You want to know the truth? Ready the truth.

The Sorbies

A long drive south
    down the coast
        to the tool store.
My first time—two guys from the crew,
    Willie the dirty biker,
        we called him,
and then the burly Will who lived
    on an old short sloop
        he sailed down from San Francisco.
And Donny, of course, my "master,"
    who I pestered
        to get me the job.
Sometimes they just liked to look at the tools,
    Will told me, and hold them,
        sometimes you have to hold them.
Like the five Sorby chisels in the broken package,
    bevel-edged, cradled in their
        cardboard stays.
Don picked the one-inch up where the shank tapers
    into the leather, into the wood,
        a beige going to yellow,
and squinted at the blade.
    "These'd be good for you," he said,
        "They're on sale,"
and handed it over handle first. And then,
    "I don't know, maybe beech,"
        when I asked
of what golden bough they were carved.

Make an Offer

Patience is the thing to remember: sooner or later it will
   be time for them to let go of what once was precious.
When they counter with a compromise, lower your bid; when
   they counter again with your original price, go even lower.
You can still lose, Father. You can still get what you want.

On Wood or Bone

There is a man in a place that is secret. He moves
   among us and keeps his riches unknown. He believes
in privacy, in silence, in swinging his elbows, in whatever
   is not readily understood—which must be magic, which
must be the thing we die with. These poems are his.

Chisel

This was the time he came down the gang-way,
        as always—
                pigeon-toed, hunched forward a little,
signing the book at 6:30
        before heading up for coffee—
            Time & Materials
as he taught me.
        I was early to the boat to cut bungs
            and grind some tools
for easy time. But the wheel had gone
        undressed for awhile
            and its rocky surface
rattled and jarred my
        precious Sorbies.
            I raised the one-inch
to him who I'd seen do almost anything
        with what he had on-hand,
            his open palm
flipped up from the swing of his arm in a sort
        of impatience, a tuck
            forming on the side of his mouth,
"Here's what you do," he said.
        Such a slow, steady, even motion left
            to right over the tough grit
of the undressed wheel,
        then he stopped,
            his wild plume of a moustache
lifting off a half-smile, and held the right corner
        still
            against the growling stone—
a full second, then another. Even I knew
        to wince at this,
            though it kept me from speaking,
watching the brown flower of burned steel
        fan across the edge and toward the shank.
            I don't think

   that iridescent bloom or the smirk I later recognized
       is why Donny died flying from my car,
           nor do I think
that is why we were such good friends.

Apologia

You can't say that you don't have one. You can't say
   that you want to change the world. You cannot affect
people or say what you learned; no one cares. Nor is it
   enough that you care. It is not enough to say anything.
You will lose your life, and you must. Men die miserably.

Forever

                    comes in its twisted figure eight

And you find five ways to fish a nymph in the swift—up, across
   and up, across, down and across, and down. You mend the drag,
or lift the rod, or jig your fly like an adult coming up for good.
   It's got to be what's under the rocks; it's got to be what's
in the weeds. Cross back under the riffle. Wait. Begin again.

Elegy

Look at my door: in every swirl of grain
   there is an image, there is a putting on
of hats: this, here, the face of an old woman
   who knows more than just my name, and
that, the chin of an old man; look how the deep
   bend betrays his concentration; he has lived
a long time, and each morning I open all
   of his dejection and pass my ever-darkening
hands across the scold marks of his years.

At one point or another you will come
   to know one path or another, abstracted to a spray
of cross-grain hyphenations: these are a flock
   of dark birds that turns and dives at once. See?
you go with them, dreaming of your woods back home,
   thinking of your fatherland again, swearing to your
motherland again. Yes, that is the brown flag
   of your country tilted in a charge, and that, the leg
of the glorious majorette you always knew.

She is still alone, and still waits for you, her fragrance
   exactly as you remember. And she still climbs
the bluff each day ... *a girl almost* ... who once braced
   a field of poppies with long and slender arms
and folded her too tender bones upon themselves—
   to think not of ruins chiseled with forgone regrets
but of when you were lost to her and of that first
   day after, when her roses trailed their petals
on still-frosted rocks and trees that now and ever
   misintend all her love and all our loving, careless youth.

Devotion

Someone or something is with you, watching or guarding
  or asking you to sleep, asking you to bring back that speck
of light always moving off to the deep periphery of your vision,
  and so you do, only to follow it back and to the left, where
someone or something waits as you shake your head No, and No.

Birth of the Father

Her long dress means what any long dress means:
  all elegance, all grace, wondrous disinterest.
The tall field is a tall field. She is in it. She is Mary.
  Her son is not Christ, though he brings light to the father.
He ushers in the great sound that bursts the heart.

Sea Voyage

> *lofdædum sceal*
> *in mægþa gehwære   man geþeon.*

Came we then down to the boat
the first time we took her out—
and Michael Mulaka writing on her stern
with electrical tape in block letters
whatever Marvin called her.
We called her Tubby, brought
the spinnakers down two men to a bag.
And Mulaka writing 'Summerland,'
where there is no port.
Ffty-two feet and beamy, she was
a fishing ketch from the Great Lakes
we covered in teak, and raised spruce masts.
It was me went up the main in the boatswain chair
to free the weather vane. It was Mike who swept
all morning—teak scraps and tack cloth.
Then we boxed and stowed tools in galley benches—
charging the time for tool maintenance,
as he taught me, on the day of the sail.
Willy was doing the rigging.
Donny was talking up the boat to Marvin.
This was tradition. We had all joined up
through Donny—he was crew chief
and the chief leads his men to the ship,
and the ship waits moored, and they make it ready.

Then they depart, voyage on the sea,
and after a time, arrive to encounter
a coast guard, a noble lord.
And men prosper in every tribe by glorious deeds.
Came we then down to the ship.
José the varnisher was pissed to lose a day of work.
The low rumble of diesel pulled us out
from the dock and through the harbor
to the higher water of the channel.

Straight up the coast into a west wind,
we keeled rails to the water and estimated
nine knots, tight sails and extended tell-tales,
except when the wind didn't die
and we lost speed. It was Willy
who went down and shouted for us stop.
It was him who left the through-hulls open.
Marvin let loose the helm and leaned against the mizzen.
Donny stopped bracing against the life line
as the boat tilted up to a full stop.
He stood straight up on the deck, head down,
hands in his pockets, hiding a half-smile
under his moustache. Everyone was turning
away from Willy, or shaking their heads,
and Willy turned below to start the pump.
With the motor submerged, a fifty-two foot ketch
under sail through the harbor, maneuvering to its slip,
the short way we came was a long way back,
the slap of water lapping in the bilge.

Ever Ending

Come, let's mourn the dead father:
   look, he is waving hello, or goodbye,
his palm inward: his job is done, or isn't:
   his body is fading, and you are the dog
that barks and barks, paws braced on the hardpan.

Eulogia

Bury the ax; bury the bow saw; bury him
   who would split my son in two, old enemy
of the wood. Let rust return to earth
   and vein the rose. Let the juniper spread
red boughs. Let indifference fester, then feed.

for my father

Aubade for Brenda

That next morning of my recuperation
    your head floated
        through a crack
in the door head-high in the haze
    of my morning vision
        and gazed
for what must have been minutes—
    looking at what
        in me?—
until I realized I was awake
    and the fear I had
        only imagined
as a child looking at the small dark
    ceramic bust
        of Eurydice
on the shelf of the next door neighbor's
    became suddenly real
        and I shouted,
and the fear deepened as it
    showed on your face
        and you came into me—
your whole body—
    and sat on the foldout bed,
        and then I calmed
of the only real fear that you are
    the only real witness of
        so far.

Never Experience

> *What evil, what unspeakable crime*
> *Have you made your life worth?*
> W. D. Snodgrass

You might never experience, nor be able to reproduce,
even from newspaper microfiche—I've seen

those pictures—what I have as memory, or mistake
for memory but what may be only facts. I saw

the tread mark on my way to the curb and not
in the police photographs strategically sprawled

across the desk of the investigating officer who saved
my wallet. "You don't want to see these." I might

reproduce for you Donny's glistening lips, the wild
moustache, thin hair across the head. But I cannot

show you with a gesture the sound of his bark,
his sip of scotch, his descent of the gangway in the morning,

an expression on his face that meant one thing to me
and another to him. That's the damned thing about it.

I have changed my life. His childhood
friend assured me that if it wasn't me, it would have been

someone else. But Donny dies everyday. A mother, if she lives,
continues to mourn. And I continue to remember.

In Memoriam

All our relatives have turned to roses
   in my mother's yard, as has my child.
They bloom out of turn. They move and speak
   with their own wag and petal-drop.
Eglantine dries on the fence. The Old Moss goes wild.

'Circe's This Craft'

A Ghost Ode on the Occasion of a Gift

And this was the time we saw her masts
   first, main and mizzen, long, solid and spruce and tilted
a little to port, her sheets twisted
     but still sagging like loose bow-strings or the tie-down of a catapult
       swinging frayed in no breeze. This Circe
         was limping through the harbor
      from age, a bad plank, and rotten ribs
        that he would sister. He'd bend
        thin strips of oak to jigs

made by shaping a thin ply template
   to get the curve inside the hull and then, by using
that, set up some clamping blocks, firmly,
     on a heavier board onto which he'd bend and clamp the strips of oak
       softened by scalding water. He'd let
        them stay for days in the sun
         drying into a shape carried down
          from the boat, then he'd glue them
          up in the same jig. It

all translates; how he'd fit it and make
   it and shape it and fit it more precisely to ex-
tend far enough beyond the rotten
     place in the existing rib to give it strength. Some call it "coupling,"
       but the proper term is "sistering,"
        as he taught me, and I used
        the technique once on a curved rafter.
         But now I'm interested
         in another Circe;

at least, I call her that, probably
   because of the first one, though she's not an actual yawl
like the first one; instead, she's a steam
     ship passenger cruiser model made by my friend John Albert Casey.
       The boat he carved me is more of an

        interpretive act than an
       imitative one. It's probably
         made of much softer wood
         than oak or African

mahogany. Its five black smoke stacks
   rise out of two tiers of upper decks (white and speckled
with black felt-tip-pen port holes) which rest
     on a two-toned hull, black and white with speckles; but what's interesting
       is the sort of folk symbol the ship
        is mounted on by way of
       two pencil-thin dowels. It's a long
        two-dimensional side view
         of a crow or raven

which began as just a base, but since
   it began to look like a bird, he went ahead and
carved it into one, then with dowels
    again, he has it all slightly raised off a larger torpedo-shaped
      base of blue sea under which he wrote
        our names and date and some care-
       fully selected lines from Dylan
        Thomas: that was one surprise.
        But there was another.

The two-tiered upper decks rattled when
   he handed it to me. It was one piece that lifted
to expose a green inner chamber
    which held a long skinny golden figure, his features roughly carved out.
       "He has a little butt," Casey said,
        as if to draw attention,
       humorously, away from the real
        idea that craft is at once
        making and mourning.

Poetry as a Way of Talking to Others

Clearly, it never works, even if they read. After a few casts
   in one pool you change your fly, you see deeper water
upstream, you see cover and a shady place where you can
   hide behind the drift, where you can make your presentation,
step out a little and let your wet fly swing, alive, under the bank.

Stealth

Down in the reeds a sucker corpse wags in the drift,
   white belly flash in the dead of evening. I'm still
for a parachute cast just above the low riffle—fly before tippet,
   before leader, before line. Some dark mass starts pushing
the sucker to shore. It doesn't know I'm there, or doesn't care.

Posse

Ye rosebuds for an old nickel it's made
  of the original material of the earth
from radical deaggregation the soft wet tissues
  from warblers for the whole genus of blackbirds
downy mullen trillium prickly ash and pine

I I

Scapulimancy

> *Earth, with your darker burdens,*
> *Drag me back down,*
> *Sink my being into my being:*
> *Sleep, sleep.*
> 　　　　　Jorge Guillen, James Wright, trans.

Divide, Divide

After the half-light
of early thermometer
readings and the months
of graphing the rise and fall

of possibility, we arrive
at the place where the body
turns in on itself and springs
into its deep action (or sinks)

and wants to sleep beyond
even our will for it—this happens
for the man too—and so we do, together,
or, me on the one couch, with you,

across the room, on the other.

Privilege

The first one, they say, is a gift; it appears
    on the end of your line. But you know a trout
is a slender muscle; you learn how it takes the nymph,
    how it attends the deep runnel, how it strikes
in the break, and you hardly lift, which is a gift.

Old English Poem

Her desire: to seek us separately who bear a soul;
    not of heaven, not of earth, here then not,
her wish for us to sound more like us than we did before,
    that we may begin to banish our own names
from our mouths with such melancholy, and such apology.

Another Old English Poem

A warrior is on the earth, brought forth from speechless
    love, which remains, in its way, which covers him,
which he obeys well, which he exalts, which, unless pride
    overcomes him, he'll reward with grace. Without a word,
a little son ambles toward his father raising his arms.

Reverdie

Let the calf pit the turf and break the bright-cheeked bud.
    Let the warm tufts brace your instep. Let the boy run, too
small to bead with dew. Still now, still now, shimmering
    not dripping, steady. His sharp shoulder bones disappear
into his raised arms. He's jumping the calf; no, the moon—

Mother's Day

A necklace of course, first choice, with beads,
    or a car, a shirt and a car, or an arm,
a pretend arm.... The animals in the book
    or on the show are lost. He can't see
their mother, so they can't—a necklace, of course.

Struck

Under the silver-leafed maple, my house
   gleams; inside, my one-year-old.
In any breeze the tree shimmers
   wagging underleaf to overleaf.
A white light burns in a pure wind.

Ever Ending

This hammer, this bear, this cloud, this ball
   this red, this mill, this tower, fins, and purple brook,
these paper ears, this paper brick, this shirt, this book,
   this car, this red car, these clothes, this handful of balloons,
all these books, all my thinking, all my tragedy:

Runian

    —OE *v. to whisper;* run, *n. whisper, mystery, secret counsel.*

Whisper this one. Small brown trout attend the weeds;
    brookies wave with the cutbank mosses. The holsteins
move off to the other side of the coulee. And you—
    hackle of pheasant, pipe felt and bead—pace up-stream.
Still, the silent dew, the small browns, the nymph descending.

    II
Something making you weep—*forecast backcast*—the last star
    recedes into the blue-jaundiced silt of dawn. The mist
accretes in the pasture. Holsteins lumber off. Something has you
    weeping. Your small son sleeps. *Forecast backcast forecast release.*
A new hatch lights on the pool, new browns rise the first time.

    III
In the deep shadow, the knee-deep water clatter, I come
    against a scrimshaw of prickly ash and barbed-wire
backlit by early yellow dawn. My nymph bounces on the roil.
    Inside that dark lacuna, a giant, a water-demon—or
a big trout. I stiffen, barb-bitten, pulled by the downy silt.

    IV
Five a.m., I'm racing a big yellow sun out of town
    to Shadow Coulee. Something's frothing in the stream,
gathering over the grassy islands, across every hanging reed.
    I'm too close yet. The browns see us coming; they can
taste our plans like a bad word, like soap in the mouth.

    V
One little brown lost to our silent scrimmage, two
    big muskrats bounding pool to pasture, three
nymphs caught in the reeds, four in the long grasses,
    five impossible tangles five times a day, five days
to fish for five fish a day, and one little brown away, away.

Scapulimancy

This is why we have two parents: all the bones
   in our chest point to the heart, to your mother gone
for the weekend, and to your little friend Theo crying
   at school. The noon-aide puts on music; she's letting him
work it out, she's letting his ribs collapse in an impossible fire.

Mantra

In the ziggurat, you fill the back of your head with a kind
   of air or calm fire. You breathe something like sound.
With each step the temple stories confine the body,
   but softer air, lighter breath, and like with water,
you move through it. You find your way to another name.

How to Deserve

what has already been given us.

Don't talk of it, make another. Don't ask. Take your fly rod
    and go deep into the pool. The sun is about to rise. Your son
is sleeping. He'll wonder where you are and what you will
    tell him. He'll wonder. He'll step slowly into the pool with you
and hear you say: "Don't talk. See the sun. Your mother is sleeping."

Poetry as a Way of Talking to the Self

Be careful what you invoke. Be careful not to ruin your mood.
    You can always lay a dry fly gently on the film, but
carefully, torque your body a little and let your light tippet
    unroll. Make your presentation and wait for the rise.
He'll be small. They grow a little at a time; they take to the air.

Ever Ending

In the time before your name becomes your mantra still
  in the time of your true name when your mother's
seems a far away taste in the fear of your half-sleep and you
  need both specters but can no longer it is morning and
because he loves you your father waits because he loves you

You, Your Mother, and I

Now the wind has died. The red wings are back to running
  off crows. The bastards. And something's chirping,
something's cooing. What's the name of that one? he says.
  You know. And nothing's worth the not looking up to see
our one, true dove huddled in the same place since winter.

Begin with a Machine

Across the way is a crane; you know it is a big machine.
    Sonja knows better. I, too, have come to know this.
She knows the crane is for lifting; she knows what it's called;
    she knows you know. She knows our motive is not
always to learn, but to teach a bright thing about ourselves.

for Jensen at age 3

To Step Out of My Heart

                and go walking beneath the enormous sky

Is to walk the same empty space my son is walking,
    under the same enormity, as a being, and as small,
as uncertain in a place as unrelenting, umbrageous.
    In my heart where he is newly emerged,
he emerges, leans into me, and I am buoyed by light.

Posse

Blue black blue black the dove is sleeping the dove
 steady on the roof peak steady the bride
and the wagging lilacs the wagging maple the shrub
 rose the boy is under down in the soil down
there a hard crust a dandy flower a terrible chute

III

Charms

Trisomy 18

We too are three bodies, with three hearts,
   considering a fourth. What are we to learn
from this? Our children are small, and strong,
   and where the current shifts one hovers
in the back eddy—wait, this is enough, only this.

Missouri Summer

Show me—I'll do what I can.
Show me that death comes

through a chain link gate and leaves
grief beside the irises. Then show me

Grief, and how he walks by slowly
damning those who feel him pass

and damning doubly those who don't.
Show me even that a blue haze

follows him through the air
like a contrail of loneliness and despair.

I would even like Grief to stop by
once and sit with me among the tomatoes

I grew from seedlings in order
to understand a sort of contiguity,

like the one between the objective notions
of *accident* and *responsibility* and *guilt*.

What Is Rare

                                    is off before you have it anywhere.

Here I don't mean trout, poetry, or children, though
    of course it's true for them, nor do I recall this claim
for the defected unborn, nor the mother of the unborn,
    nor the delicate happiness of mothers, nor true love,
which I have, which I found in time and find easy to keep.

Reincarnation

Verso: this cold night, this cold wind, we will protect
    our possibilities by hiding them: this job,
this book, the land, our remarkable son—regret,
    another suitcase, all these damn toys, that dog.
Recto: the one we lean against, the one we knew before.

Poetry as a Way of Talking to Spirit

But already It overhears everything. Besides, you want It to speak.
   You want to catch anything you can and something big.
Dress a long hook with feathers and fur, tinsel and peacock hurl.
   Labor your streamer across the current or up. It will swing.
It will incite a deep strike. You'll have a long fight. Congratulations.

A Sort of Hunger

After the symphony of mowers and edgers
   they rise and brush the decay
of thatch—as I would. And the robin,
   the blackbird, the jay descend hurriedly
onto their lithe and brittle bodies—as I would.

Were I This Forest Pool

and you this birch tree bending over

Or, maybe a willow, with your long hair of mourning, then
   I would lie still. You lose what I cannot. The small strands
of leaves wind-raked from the branch settle and ripple out. Even
   the small trout hold in the deep. But see our boy run wildly
through the outlet riffle? There: all our joy—and deepest grief.

Blood Trout

All things being unequal, these are equal: my son asking
   where my father is, any dog barking from a leash
staked in the yard, leaving them to fish, and the brook trout
   who took my fuzzy nymph too deep in the throat. I tried
with forceps, but already blood dripped from the gills.

Com On Wanre Niht

Down to the stream, a point fly and two droppers. Maybe
    I could've had three, all unwitting and stuck in the gills.
One small boy was teaching me patience. And I hit all red lights
    going out of town; then, one deep strike on one nymph
impossible to get out, and one corpse in the drift, unrevived.

Moon and Sun

Strip rough bark from the yew and shave a slender
    bow. It guards against fire, against the waxing bullock
on the rise, horns filled with plunder from the sun.
    Sit patiently in the dark grass and dew. Your wife
and small son are sleeping. You can't know their way.

In Swaying Copse the Willows

                      wave their magic wands.

And our barely boy runs blithely through them, raising his arms,
    the small leaves to rake his naked sides. Follow what toad?
Muddy what shoes? Under what rock the crawdad? Behind him
    the lightless places brace and buoy the dense brush. He turns
back to us, armloads of willow hair. All hail to wagging sunlit leaves.

Stealth

We're told that rain brings them up indiscriminately.
    The dark swell tumbles the small mice and hoppers
and ants; the world of water and land knock loose. And they
    can't see me, I guess, splashing, rod aloft, tipping slowly
back and to the side like one of their own fry caught in the drift.

Mentor

I know you know differently:
   that the petal curls back to open inwardly,
that you can also diminish the need
   for your body, that there is such happiness.
Forgive me: I have simply forgotten who you are.

Poem for the Holidays

That baggy Missouri cypress, red-balled with a fungi—
   red-balled? rust-balled?—gelatinous, rusty balls of useless
fingers, rusty All Saints ghosts stopped melting, bunches
   of them like bad flowers, bad ornaments on a bad
Christmas cypress in our first front yard ever. I had to love it.

The Tongues of Water
>   creeping in, quietly.

Yes, in a new moon, in a dark time, I rise from sleep
    beside your smooth side. It is then that the big fish
tunnel the open water seeking out fry of their own kind
    and others, and their larger cousins. I lie not distracted
by fish, but by what the fish weaves in his reed-loom of desire.

Verse

At the edge of these torn pages—a few pines, a worn
    meadow—the cult of the gallant fox presides.
They know better: their ruthless vixens, their procreant
    vulnerabilities. Nevertheless, they assemble for the free vector
of the dog fox, and the blue-tongued omega lying down to die.

Next Dream

Colder than ever—
        and this afternoon, upstairs,
you were already kneeling,
dressed in the grey haze of rain,
imagining some child you were or woman you'll become
                        convulsing in your arms.
It must have been when you cradled
her trembling head
        and scowled a "shush" as if to me
that I shuddered before walking past your house.
"There now," I can hear you say, "sleep is better than water. . . ."

But you rarely sleep, and so I rarely see you there—
                                            yet today,
when I went home out of the rain to nap,
I saw my lips, dried and cracked like husks,
                        press to your neck
and your thin tongue hiss across fire-blackened sandstone.
Behind us my brother stood
        in place of my father,
the tail of a blue-belly lizard,
        lost in the chase,
                wagging in his hand.
He nailed it to the garage beam with other ropes.
And someone besides my father was missing,
                and the nail she hung on,
as if she was that ailing version of yourself,
was empty, and one of the ropes was gone.

Why this dream tonight with someone like you who hardly sleeps?
Why only now,
        do you lift your face
from the wild gaze of the woman you contained so long
behind locked wrists
        and turn to me, slowly, finally?
Coldest of Sundays—
there must be a tremendous recovery in my future.

Enskyment

To be taken up by birds, as a fish by an osprey
   or a man on a hillside by a vulture, or a salamander
by a crow, if a crow desires it. In this way the prey
   lifts the predator by the beak, and as we rise
in that tilt, a wan light glances off the blacks of our eyes.

No Name

And no dark day. Just two black hearts under the green leaves
   and blue sky. Our boy Jensen asks: can we go to the park
when it's yellow? And when bright twilight comes, we go,
   one of us pushing him on the one swing, the other sitting
on the other, to keep it from moving, to keep it absolutely still.

Oracle Bones

I see you abducted—a woman with black hair leads you
   across a road, her black bag hangs like a sleeping hand.
I ask your names, snatch the purse and bring her down.
   I hold my own shoulder over the flames and read the lines—
what will is what was. It can be bleak; it can bring us hope.

Posse

Can you finish can you be burned together can you wake
  to a prairillian of grey feathers to the black beads
of the watchers their surveillant indifference their caws their
  runic impressions in the creek silt they return to their mates
they die without you they rear their young you are beholden

Charm

I cannot know what that crow says
   but I would warrant that it is nothing
incidental, nothing that can wait,
   and nothing that we need to know
before this one last turn around the block.
   The doctor is waiting with some news.
It used to be a doctor was a teacher, he'd teach
   us how to keep our bodies well, he'd help
fill our minds to feed our hearts. But now
   we have a phone call, now we have
to be ready for anything. There are procedures
   to explain, and something like odds.
Chances are, what the crow says is pertinent,
   but in this foot-full of leaves we brush aside
lies any number of possibilities and at least one
   alley we have never considered before.
We have little time. We have little to say.
   Listen, the crow is not divine; his caw is just
perhaps, but if I call upon him as an image,
   then I declare him to be only that.
Let no black bird be anything else than that
   which comes into my musings to represent
the constant and normal, tragic and daily
   inventions that any father might imagine
when before him a perfect boy points upward
   in autumn to the same two doves perched
on the same two wires he pointed to last autumn.
   Let me now declare that this crow beckons
only what's already past, and that where our only boy
   has one brother and one little sister, neither
having suffered any kind of misery, there only
   as a dreamer shall he lay a leaf by the head
of each, and I accompany him, and I bring him
   home to wake in peace and in full being
between me his father, and her his only mother.

NOTES

THE HANDWORM'S HIPBONE: See the Old English charm against wens.

SWALLOWS: *The Exeter Book (Exeter Cath. MS. 3501)* contains the Old English riddle cycle which was edited by Craig Williamson, *The Old English Riddles of the* Exeter Book, University of North Carolina Press: Chapel Hill, 1977. All future references to the OE riddles will use his numbering. Cf. OE riddle #55.

FOREVER: Title & epigraph from "Waking at 3 A.M." by William Stafford.

MOON AND SUN: Cf. OE riddle #27; the rune, *eoh*, is the "yew" rune.

EULOGIA: Cf. OE riddle # 19 (Plow).

ON WOOD OR BONE: Cf. OE poem "The Husband's Message" and the reference therein to *runestæfas*.

APOLOGIA: Epigraph from "The Pink Locust" by William Carlos Williams.

SEA VOYAGE: Beowulf ll.24b-25, translated in the poem, line 28.

OLD ENGLISH POEM: Cf. OE riddle #37 (Speech); OE *v. wrecan* means "to utter" and "to banish."

ANOTHER OLD ENGLISH POEM: Cf. OE riddle # 48 (Fire).

SCAPULIMANCY: "the heating of bones to produce cracks which are interpreted as oracular signs" Wu Jing-Nuan, *Yi Jing*, The Taoist Center: WDC, 1991, p.11. Usually employs the scapula of a bull, or in North America (Canada), that of a caribou.

HOW TO DESERVE: Title & epigraph from "Love in the Country" by William Stafford.

TRISOMY 18: Also known as Edward Syndrome after the doctor who discovered this genetic defect. This occurs when the 18th chromosome has three bodies. A fetus rarely lives to birth with this defect, and, if born, will be severely mentally retarded and usually die within the first year of life.

WHAT IS RARE: Title & epigraph from "Sonnet on Rare Animals" by William Meredith.

REINCARNATION: recto is the right side page of a book's bifolio; verso is the back of it, the subsequent left side.

WERE I THIS FOREST POOL: Title & epigraph from "Words" by C. Day Lewis.

COM ON WANRE NIHT: "He/She came in the dark night" *Beowulf* (702 b).

IN SWAYING COPSE THE WILLOWS: Title & epigraph from "Words" by C. Day Lewis.

TO STEP OUT OF MY HEART: Title & epigraph from "Lament" by Rilke, Stephen Mitchell, trans.

THE TONGUES OF WATER: Title & epigraph from "Meditations at Oyster River" by Theodore Roethke.

ENSKYMENT: after Jeffers.

ORACLE BONES: See note to "Scapulimancy" above.

CHARM: See the Old English charm against wens.

Printed in the United States
200209BV00002B/1-45/A